For The Children

Words of Love and Inspiration from His Holiness Pope John Paul II

Scholastic Press

Callaway

2000

Greeting

 greet you with my whole heart,
and I tell you that you bring me particularly great joy.
One is always happy among the young.

The Pope wishes well to everyone,
but he has a preference for the youngest,
because they had a special place
in the heart of Christ,
who wished to remain with the children
and to talk to the young.

He addressed his call to the young especially,
and John, the youngest apostle,
was his favorite.

General Audience in St. Peter's Basilica with ten thousand children, Vatican City

The Gospel of Children

ow important children are in the eyes of Jesus!
We could even say that the *Gospel is full of the truth about children*.
The whole of the Gospel could actually be read as the "Gospel of children."

What does it mean that "unless you turn and become
like children, you will not enter the kingdom of heaven"?
Is not Jesus pointing to children as models even for grown-ups?

In children there is something that must never be missing
in people who enter the kingdom of heaven. People who
are destined to go to heaven are simple like children,
and like children are full of trust, rich in goodness and pure.

Only people of this sort can find in God a Father and,
thanks to Jesus, can become in their own turn children of God.

Letter of the Pope to Children, Vatican City

Hope

repare for life
with seriousness and diligence.

Always remember that only if one builds,
as St. Paul says,
on the one foundation
which is Jesus Christ,
will one be able to construct
something really great and lasting.

With the liveliness that is characteristic of your age,
with the generous enthusiasm
of your young hearts,
walk towards Christ.

He alone is the solution
to all your problems.

He alone is the way,
          the truth
             and the life;

he alone is the real salvation
of the world;
he alone is the hope of mankind.

Speech to eight thousand children in Guadalajara, Mexico

Love

eople cannot live without love. They are called to love God and their neighbor, but in order to love properly they must be certain that God loves them.

God loves you, dear children! This is what I want to tell you. . . .

Letter of the Pope to Children, Vatican City

rue happiness lies in giving ourselves in love to our brothers and sisters.

Message to young people in Camagüey, Cuba

Love

irst of all,
I tell you that Jesus loves you!
This is the truth that the Vicar of Christ
proclaims to you:
Jesus loves you!

I hope that there are so many persons
who love you and I earnestly trust
that each one of you
is happy,
finding kindness, affection
and understanding
in all and from all.

But we also must be realistic. . . .
And so it may often happen
that one feels in one's heart
a sense of emptiness,
loneliness, sadness
and discontent.

One may even have everything,
but be missing joy!

Above all, it is terrible to see
so much suffering,
so much poverty,
so much violence.

Well, in this drama of life
and of human history,
the message of the Gospel
sounds out: Jesus loves you!
Jesus came to this earth
to show us
and to guarantee to us
God's love.
He came to love us
and to be loved.

Let yourselves be loved by Christ!

Speech to children in the Church of
San Basilio, Rome, Italy

10

Prayer

f you follow Jesus' advice and pray to God
constantly, then you will learn to pray well.
God himself will teach you.

Meeting with youth in New Orleans, Louisiana

13

Prayer

What enormous power the prayer of children has!
This becomes a *model for grown-ups themselves*:
praying with simple and complete trust means praying as children pray.

It is to your prayers that I want to entrust the problems of your own families
and of all the families in the world.
And not only this: I also have other intentions to ask you to pray for.
The Pope counts very much on your prayers.
We must pray together and pray hard,
that humanity, made up of billions of human beings,
may become more and more the family of God and able to live in peace.

[There is] unspeakable suffering which many children have experienced
in this century, and which many of them are continuing to endure
at this very moment. How many of them, even in these days,
are becoming victims of the hatred which is raging in different
parts of the world: in the Balkans, for example, and in some African countries.

It was while I was thinking about these facts, which fill our hearts with pain, that I decided to ask you, dear boys and girls, to take upon yourselves the duty of *praying for peace*. You know this well: *love and harmony build peace, hatred and violence destroy it.*

You instinctively turn away from hatred and are attracted by love: for this reason the Pope is certain that you will not refuse his request, but that you will join in his prayer for peace in the world with the same enthusiasm with which you pray for peace and harmony in your own families.

Letter of the Pope to Children, Vatican City

Faith

od calls every person,
and his voice makes itself heard
even in the hearts of children:
he calls people to live in marriage or to be priests;
he calls them to the consecrated life
or perhaps to work in the missions. . . .
Who can say?
Pray, dear boys and girls,
that you will find out what your calling is,
and that you will follow it generously.

Letter of the Pope to Children, Vatican City

Family

llow me
to enter your homes;
yes, you want to have the Pope
as your guest and friend,
and to give him the consolation
of seeing in your homes
the union and the family love
which gives rest,
after a hard day's work.

It shows me, dear children,
that you are preparing seriously
for the future;

I repeat to you,
you are the hope of the Pope.

Do not deny me the joy
of seeing you walk along paths
that lead you
to be real followers of good,
and friends of Christ.

Do not deny me the joy
of your sense of responsibility
in studies, activities
and amusements.

You are called to be bearers
of generosity and honesty,
to fight against immorality,
to prepare a more just,
healthier and happier world.

Speech to one hundred thousand families in Guadalajara, Mexico

In the family . . . husband and wife, adults and children, brothers and sisters accept one another as God's gift and give each other the life and love of God. In the family the healthy and sick stand by each other. Young and old speak up for one another. They try to solve problems together. . . . Lastly, the family is also the place where everyone can experience mutual forgiveness in an atmosphere of love.

Discourse to the Schönstatt Family Association, Vatican City

School

ear students,

Hold school in esteem! Return to it joyfully; consider it a great gift, a fundamental right which, of course, also involves duties.

Think of all your contemporaries in many countries of the world who have no education at all. *Illiteracy is a plague, a heavy "handicap,"* which comes in addition to that of hunger and other miseries. With illiteracy, not only is some aspect of the economy and political life at issue, but the *very dignity of the human being.* The right to education is the right to be fully human.

Best wishes, then, dear students!

Angelus prayer, Castel Gandolfo, Italy

Holidays

He rests well who works well and,
in his turn, he who works well must rest well.

Enjoy your holidays!
But make them also a period
of constant and courageous effort
to become better.

Let your play,
your stay in the mountains
or the seaside,
your trips,
your carefree joyfulness,
always be united
with the resolution to be good,
in friendship with Jesus in the Eucharist.

May my prayer and my blessing
accompany you.

Take advantage of this period of rest
to strengthen your spirit too.

Try with the help of divine grace
always to be good, joyful and generous.

Speech in St. Peter's Square, Vatican City

Violence

I appeal to young people
who may have become caught up
in groups who do violence.

I say to you,
with all the love I have for you,
with all the trust I have in young people:
do not listen to voices which speak
the language of hatred,
revenge, retaliation.

Do not follow any leaders
who train you in the ways of causing death.

Love life, respect life,
in yourselves and in others.
Give yourselves to the service of life,
not the work of death.

Do not think that courage and strength
are proved by killing and destruction.

True courage lies in working for peace.

Speech to children in Drogheda, Ireland

Peace

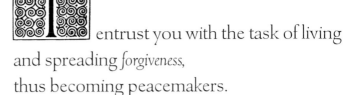

I entrust you with the task of living
and spreading *forgiveness,*
thus becoming peacemakers.

Looking at the crib, where the little Child
lies in the straw of the manger,
we can easily understand what forgiveness is:
it is reaching out to the other who offended me,
coming close to him who drew away from me.

God was faithful to sinful humanity
to the point of dwelling among us. . . .

The Son of God loved us, who offended him,
and thus conquered evil with his good.

To hate sin but to love the sinner:
this is the way to peace,
the way that the Lord teaches us
from the mystery of his birth.

When I look at you, boys and girls,
I see, as it were, Jesus' peers.

Christmas Greeting to Catholic Action Children, Vatican City

Suffering

I want all sick children everywhere to know
that the Pope prays for each one of you.
You know how much Jesus loved children
and how pleased he was to be with them.
You too are very special to him.
Some of you and your friends have suffered a lot
and you feel the burden of what has happened to you.
I want to encourage you to be patient and to stay close
to Jesus, who suffered and died on the Cross
out of love for you and me.

And of course there are your families and friends
who love you very much and want you to be strong and brave.
I am happy to bless all of them.

I invite all the sick to trust in Jesus who said:
"I am the resurrection and the life."
In union with him, even our trials and sufferings
are precious for the redemption of the world.
May his Mother Mary accompany you
and fill your hearts with joy.

Message to the children at Cardinal Glennon Children's Hospital, St. Louis, Missouri

My First Communion

Iremember as though it were yesterday when, together with the other boys and girls of my own age, I received the Eucharist for the first time in the parish church of my town. This event is usually commemorated in a family photo, so that it will not be forgotten. Photos like these generally remain with a person all through his or her life.

As time goes by, people take out these pictures and experience once more the emotions of those moments; they return to the purity and joy experienced in the meeting with Jesus, the One who out of love became the Redeemer of man.

Letter of the Pope to Children, Vatican City

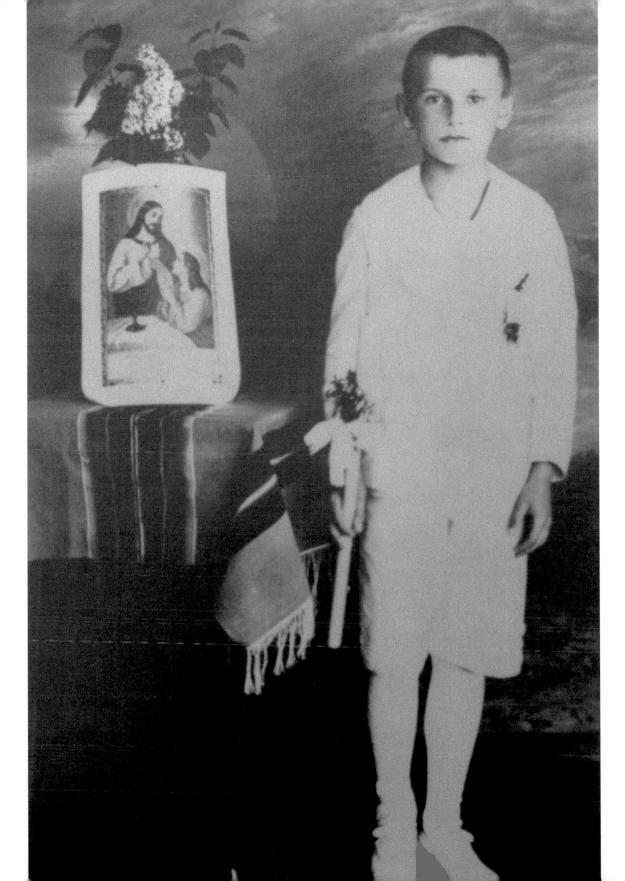

The World's Children

Dear boys and girls,

Let me recall the words of a Psalm which have always moved me: *Laudate pueri Dominum!* Praise, O children of the Lord, praise the name of the Lord! Blessed be the name of the Lord from this time forth and for evermore! From the rising of the sun to its setting may the name of the Lord be praised!

As I meditate on the words of this Psalm, the *faces of all the world's children* pass before my eyes: from the East to the West, from the North to the South. It is to you, young friends, without distinction of language, race or nationality, that I say:
Praise the name of the Lord!

Letter of the Pope to Children, Vatican City

Callaway Editions would like to gratefully acknowledge Pauline Books & Media, *L'Osservatore Romano*, Greg Burke and Elizabeth Heil.

The italicizing herein reflects emphasis contained in the original papal documents.

PHOTO CAPTIONS

p. 1 Mexico, 1990; p. 2 Vatican City, 1983; p. 5 Poland, 1987; p. 7 Prague, 1990; p. 8 Rome, 1982; p. 11 Mexico, 1979; p. 12 Pusan, South Korea, 1984; p. 15 Lodz, Poland, 1987; p. 17 Glasgow, Scotland, 1982; p. 19 Sistine Chapel, Vatican City, 1997; p. 20 Melbourne, Australia, 1986; pp. 22–23 Lourdes, France, 1983; p. 27 Darwin, Australia, 1986; p. 28 The future Pope, Karol Wojtyla, at age eleven, (front row, second from left) as an altar boy; p. 29 Karol Wojtyla at age nine, on the day of his First Communion, in 1929; pp. 30–31 From left: Vatican City, 1989; Benin, 1993; Quito, Ecuador, 1985; Poland, 1979; South Korea, 1984; p. 32 Vatican City, 1985; Front Cover: Lyons, France, 1986; Back Cover: Vatican City, 1983.

PICTURE CREDITS

© Maurizio Brambatti/Reuters/Piekna/MaxPPP: p. 19; © Catholic Press Photo: pp. 28 and 29; © Gianni Giansanti/Sygma: pp. 22–23; © Giancarlo Giuliani/Periodici San Paolo: pp. 30 (right), 31 (center), and back cover; © François Lochon/Gamma: pp. 12, 31 (left and right), and front cover; © Servizio Fotografico de *L'Osservatore Romano*: pp. 1, 2, 5, 7, 8, 11, 17, 20, 27, 30 (left); © James L. Stanfield/National Geographic Image Collection: pp. 15 and 32.

Library of Congress Cataloging-in-Publication Data available upon request.
LC # 99–37802
ISBN 0–439–14902–9

10 9 8 7 6 5 4 3 2 1
0/0 01 02 03 04

Printed in China by Palace Press International
First edition, March 2000